Christmas Caticorn
Activity Book For Kids
Ages 4-8

Copyright 2020 by Happy Harper - All rights reserved.

This document is geared towards providing exact and reliable information in regards to the topic and issue covered. The publication is sold with the idea that the publisher is not required to render an accounting, officially permitted, or otherwise, qualified services. If advice is necessary, legal or professional, a practiced individual in the profession should be ordered.

- From a Declaration of Principles which was accepted and approved equally by a Committee of the American Bar Association and a Committee of Publishers and Associations.

In no way is it legal to reproduce, duplicate, or transmit any part of this document by either electronic means or in printed format. Recording of this publication is strictly prohibited and any storage of this document is not allowed unless with written permission from the publisher. All rights reserved.

The information provided herein is stated to be truthful and consistent, in that any liability, in terms of inattention or otherwise, by any usage or abuse of any policies, processes, or directions contained within is the solitary and utter responsibility of the recipient reader. Under no circumstances will any legal responsibility or blame be held against the publisher for any reparation, damages, or monetary loss due to the information herein, either directly or indirectly.

Respective authors and companies own all copyrights not held by the publisher.

The information herein is offered for informational purposes solely and is universal as so. The presentation of the information is without a contract or any type of guarantee assurance.

The trademarks that are used are without any consent, and the publication of the trademark is without permission or backing by the trademark owner. All trademarks and brands within this book are for clarifying purposes only and are owned by the owners themselves, not affiliated with this document.

This Book Belongs to

_____

Circle the odd one in each square.

2

The caticorn is on a mission to find Christmas words. Can you help her?

```
Y M I S T L E T O E I H
K O R N A M E N T S W S
C D P C N C T O R K E A
N U F B J M W P Z W L N
P A P X X L O A P Q V T
H O L I D A Y O V M E A
T F S T O C K I N G S C
R O C F V R G I F T N L
E X A V L U M K H P G A
E Z R C T H N U W Z P U
W N O R T H P O L E Z S
D T L J C I M I E V B Q
```

MISTLETOE
CAROL
GIFT
TREE
SANTA CLAUS
NORTH POLE
ELVES
STOCKINGS
ORNAMENTS
HOLIDAY

Guide the caticorn to the top of the Christmas tree.

4 Help the caticorn count the Christmas decorations.

Help the caticorn get to the Christmas present.

What comes next?

Unscramble the words to complete the crossword.

Across
1. rohn
3. caitronc
6. irfay
7. nrtho lope
8. loracs
9. delcan
11. weom
13. vsele

Down
2. lophrud
3. chminye
4. nowairbs
5. yadolih
8. sloudc
10. lenag
12. loyjl

Use the color key to color the picture.

1 - Pink
2 - Purple
3 - Red
4 - Brown
5 - Blue
6 - Yellow
7 - Green
8 - Black
9 - White

Spot 5 differences between the pictures.

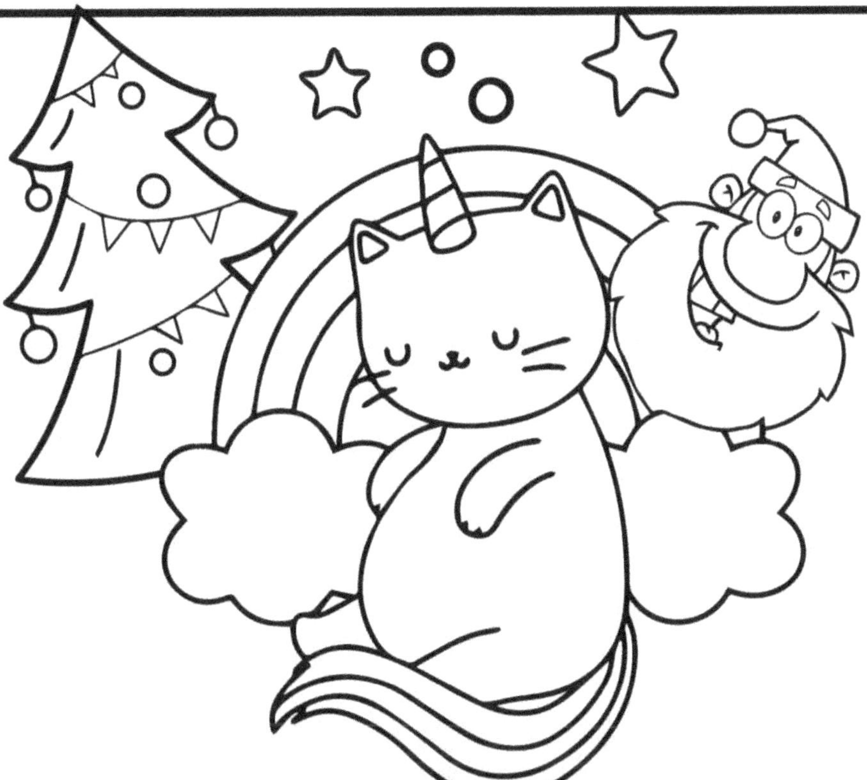

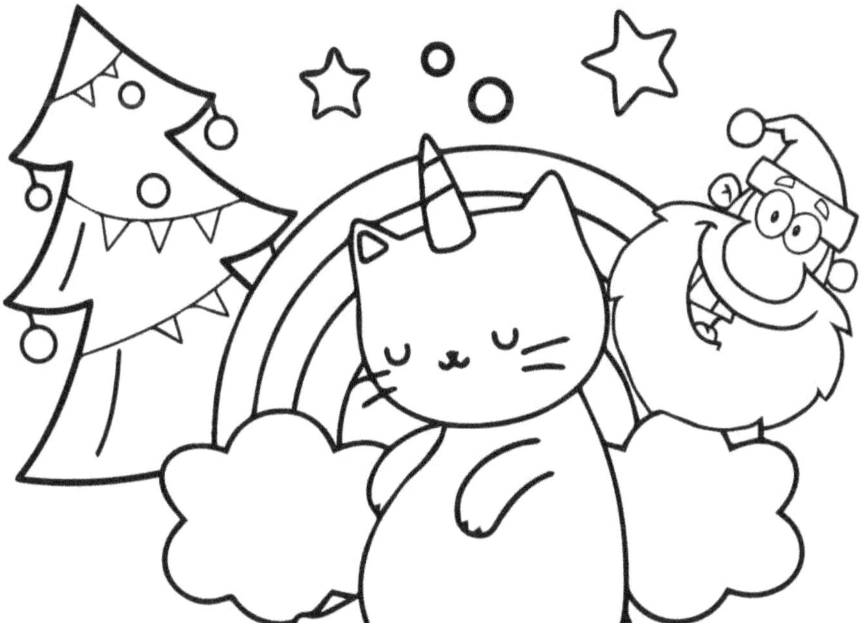

Write the correct symbol in each circle. Is it greater than, less than or equal to?

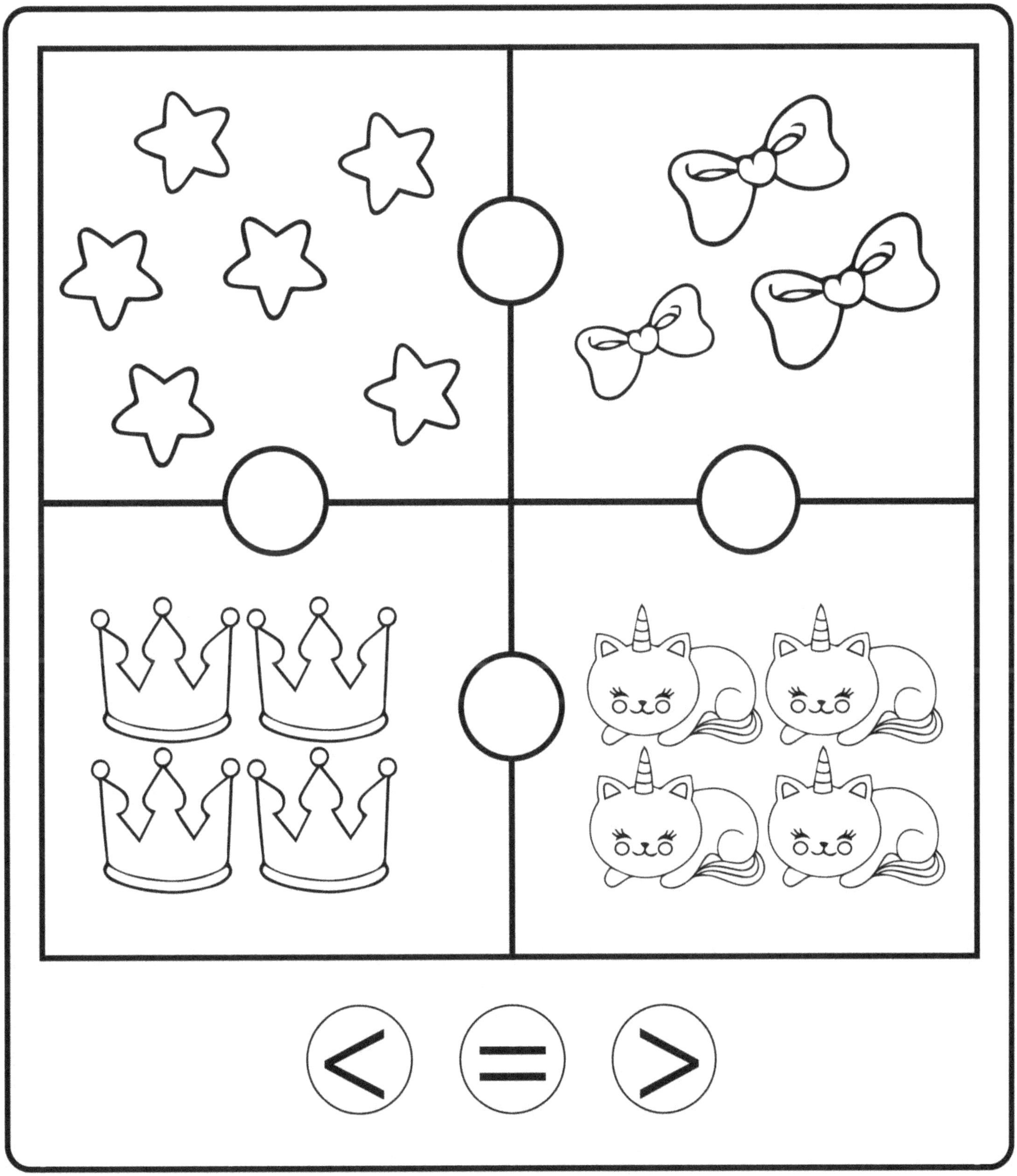

< = >

11

Find the words listed below.

```
L R E E D N I E R W E B
R E T T I L G I W H T N
S N R O C I T A C G R O
Q A R Q M W B W R I N B
U A M E L G H Y E E L N
N E N T B I I L T L A O
J O L A S M I M N S C B
P N T K M I E Z I E I H
F N E I N W R C W D T A
G R E T R I O H E X S N
S Q D R I P W N C D Y K
E G Q Y A G I T S X M Y
```

MYSTICAL   CHRISTMAS   WINTER

SLEIGH   CATICORN   SNOWMAN

REINDEER   WHISKERS   BONBON

DECEMBER   GLITTER   TWINKLE

12

Draw a line to help the caticorn match the Santa to its shadow.

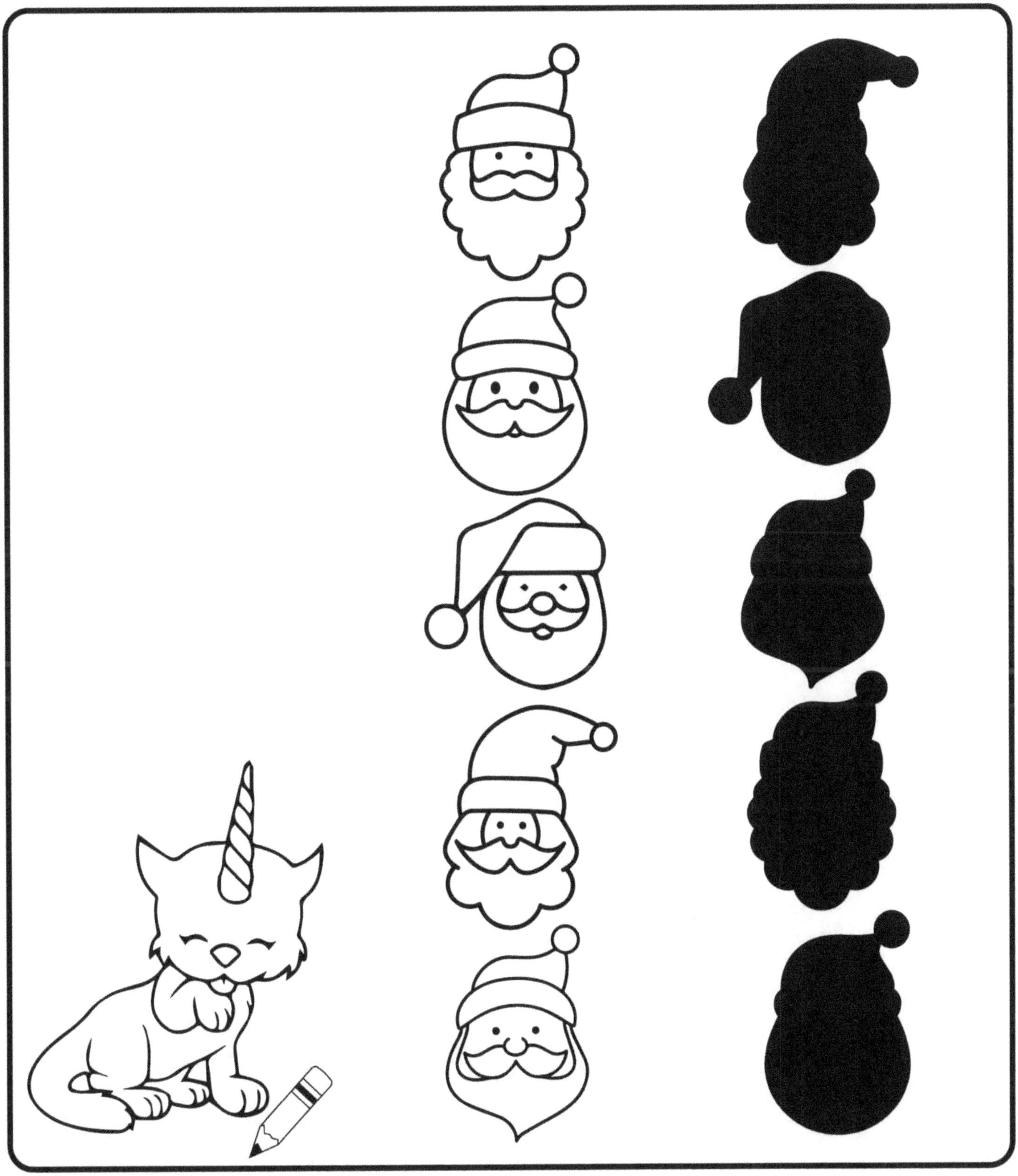

Connect the dots to complete the picture.

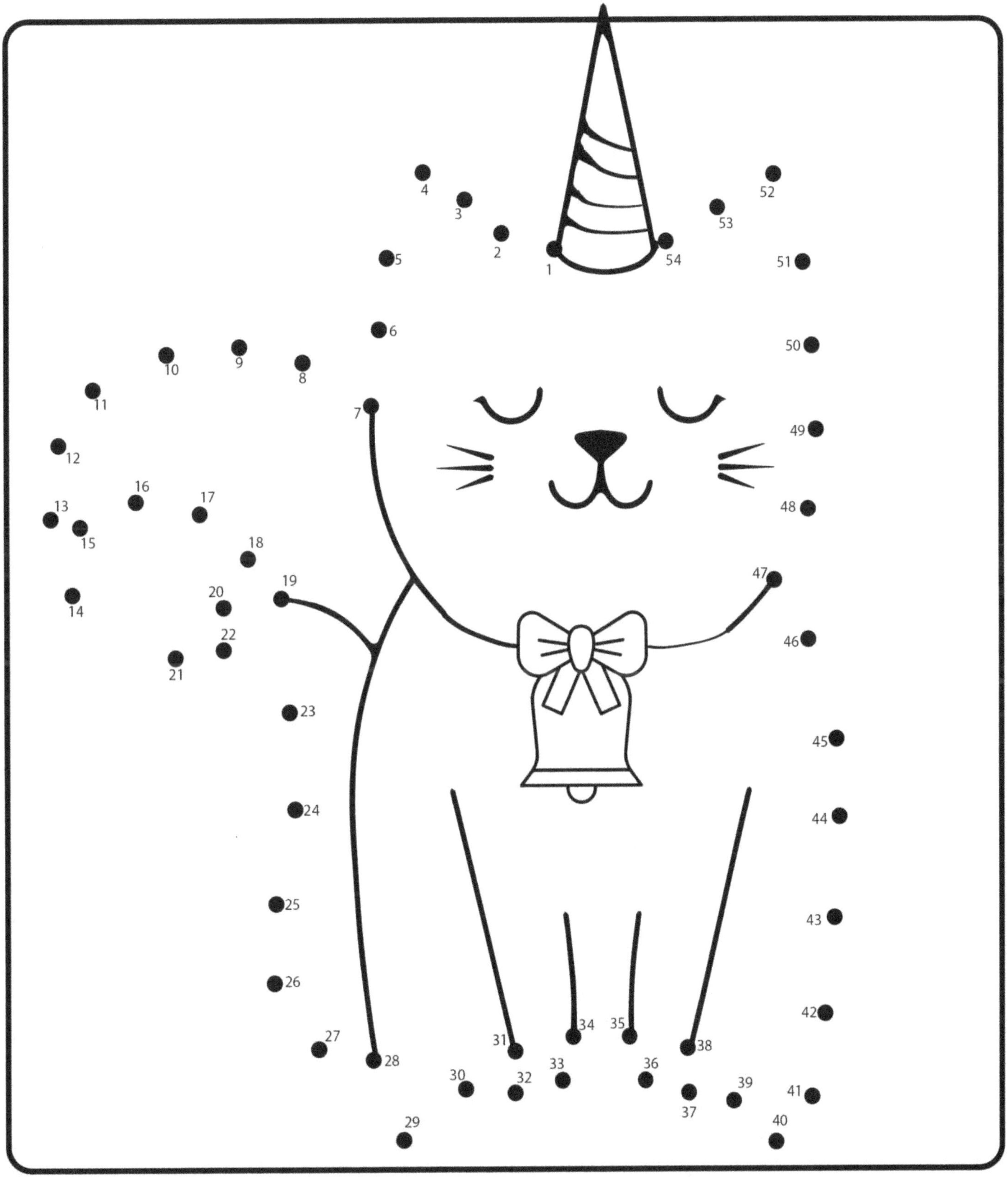

14 Can you solve the caticorn problem?

caticorn + caticorn + stocking + caticorn = ☐

cat + caticorn + cat − caticorn = ☐

cat + caticorn + bauble − caticorn = ☐

stocking + bauble + bauble − caticorn = ☐

  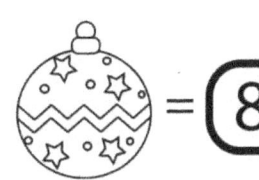

# 15
Spot 5 differences between the pictures.

The caticorn has dropped its Christmas hat. Can you help the caticorn find it?

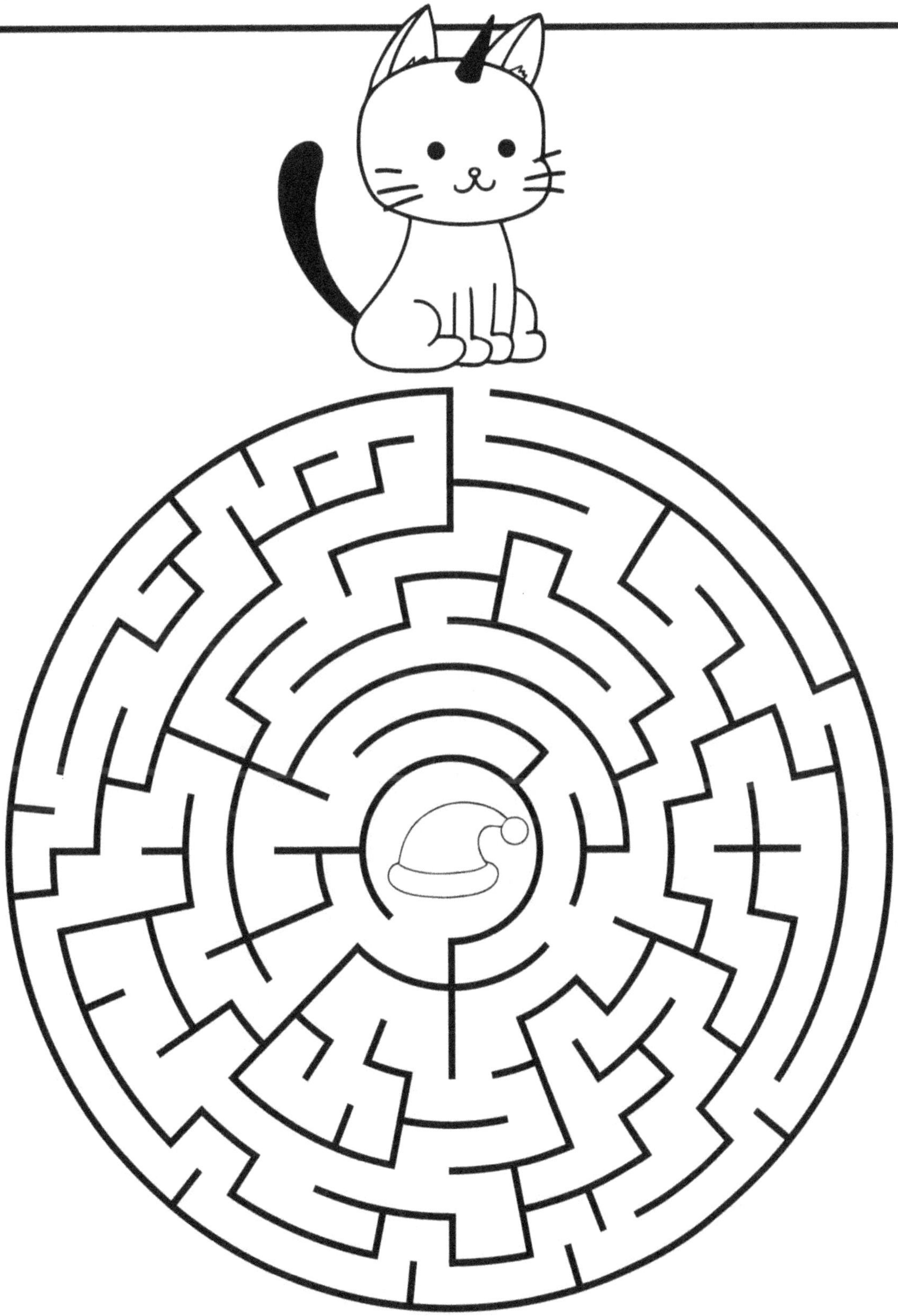

Use the color key to color the picture.

a - green
b - red
c - yellow
d - white
e - pink
f - orange
g - purple
h - brown

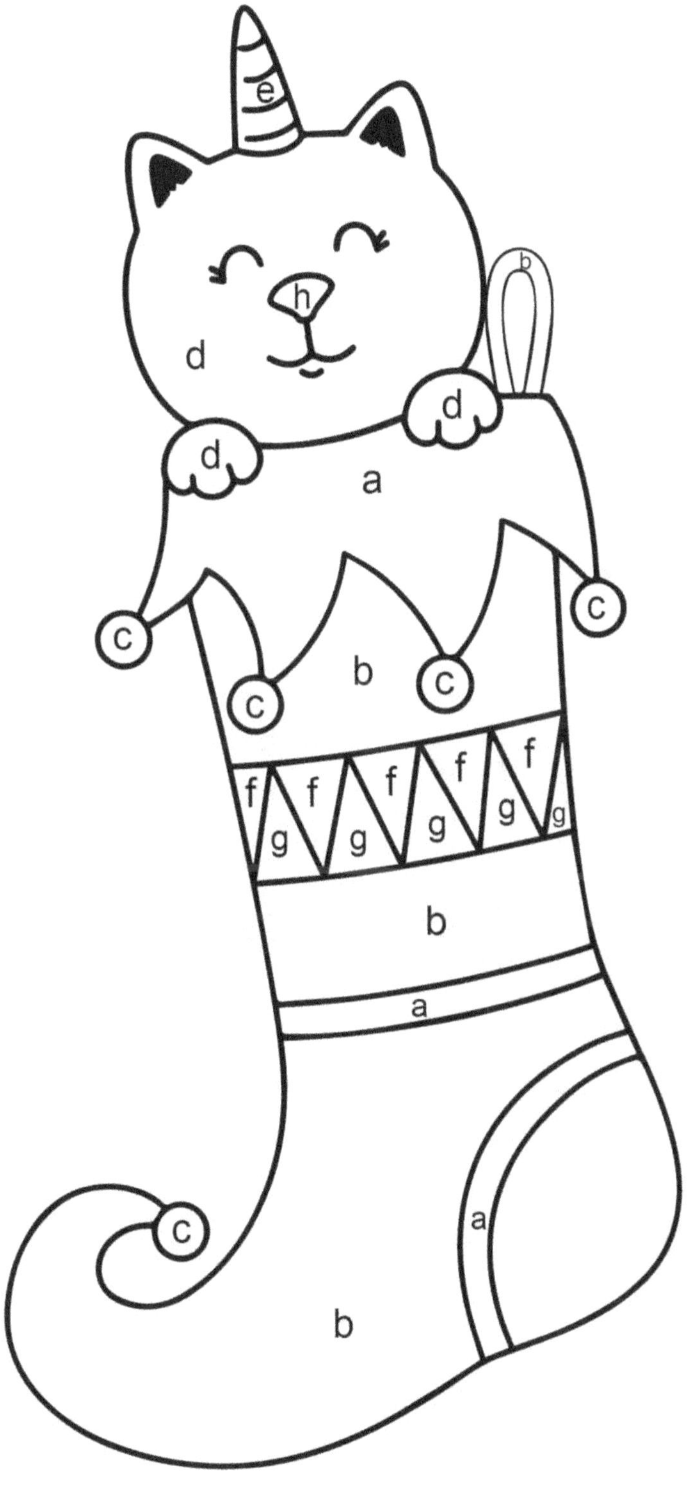

Color the objects that repeat three times in a row.

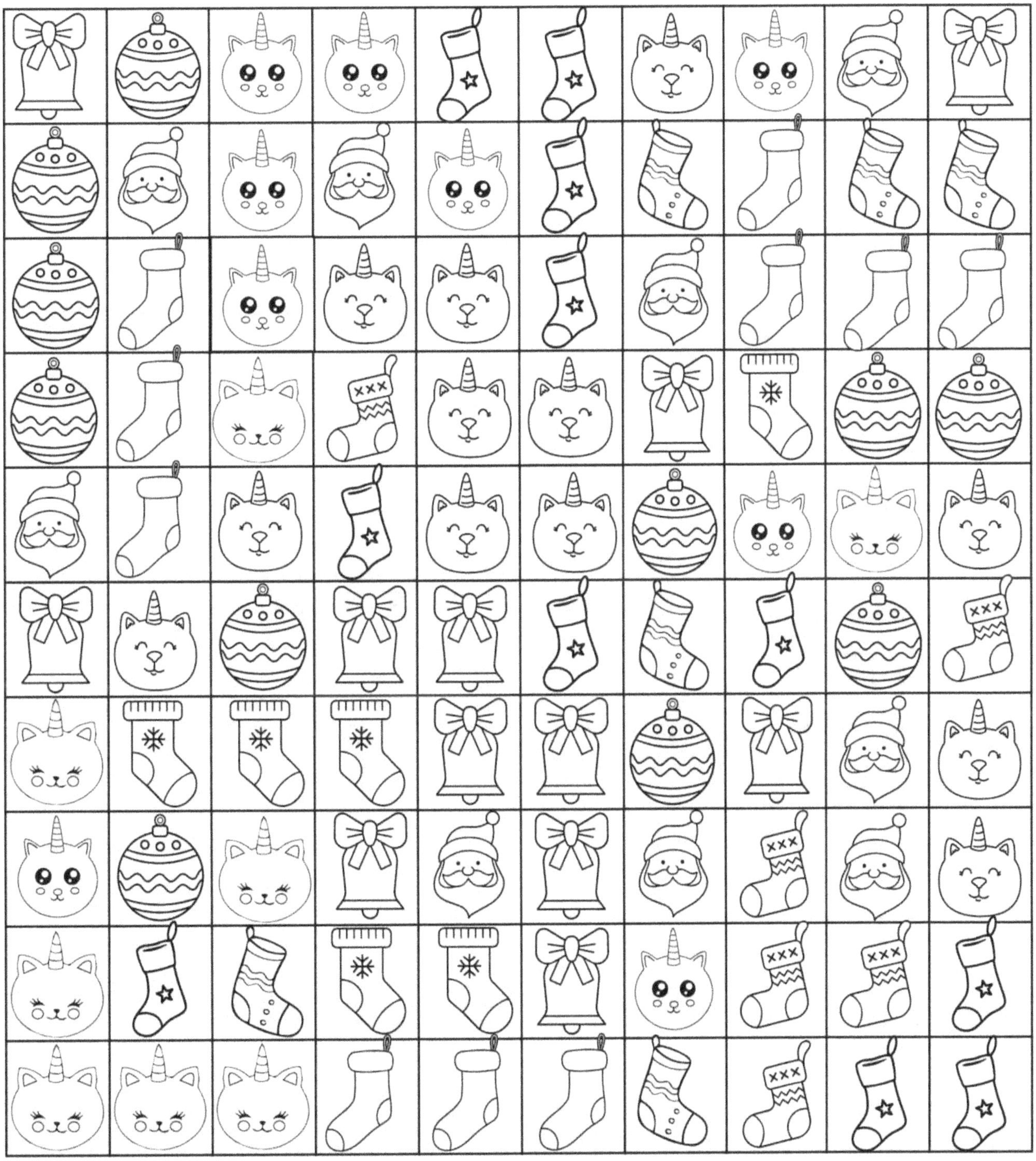

Draw the missing parts to complete the caticorn's face.

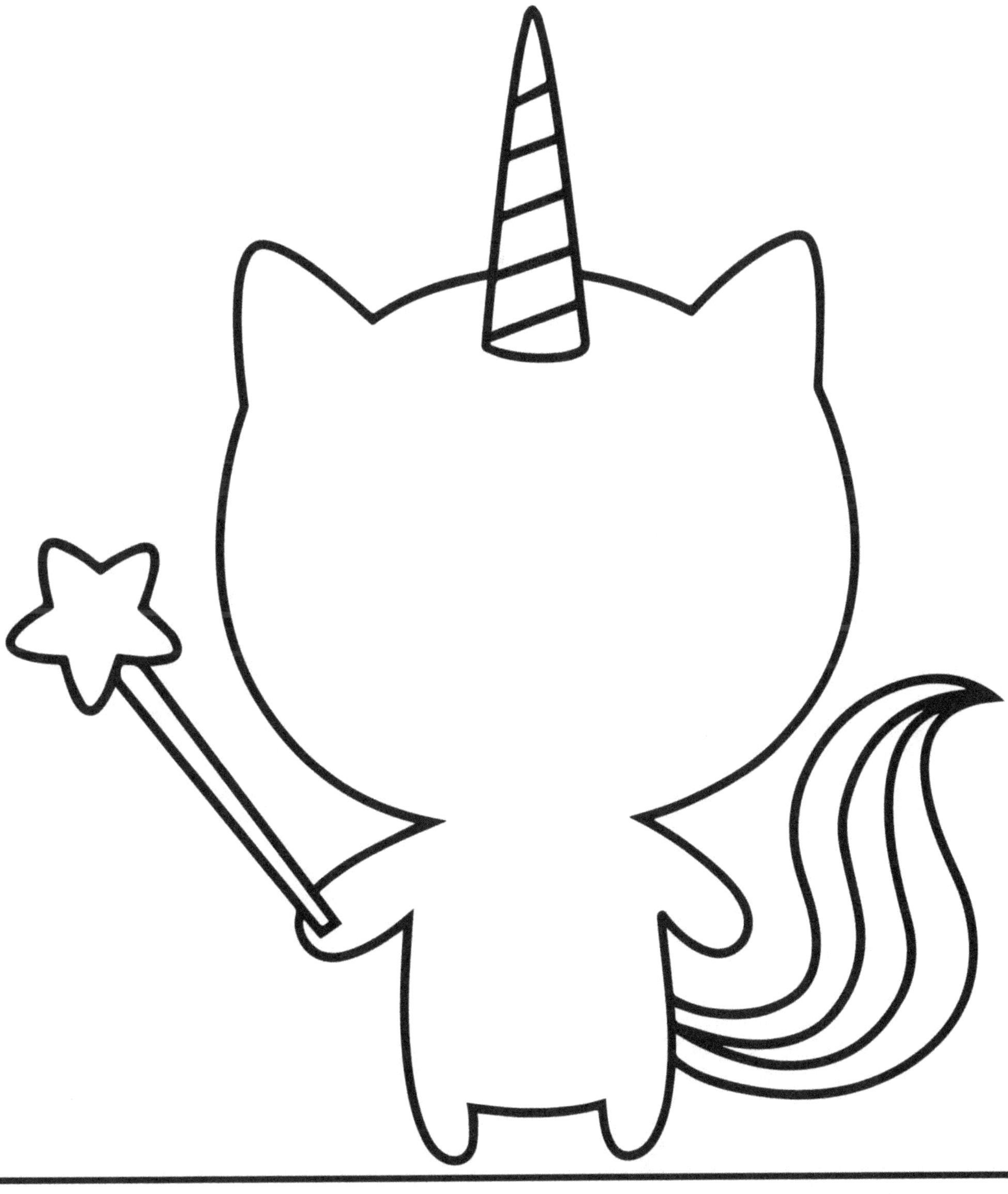

Count and color the correct number.

Awesome work on completing all the pages!
&
Merry Christmas!

(the answers to the activities are on the next few pages)

1 Circle the odd one in each square.

2 The caticorn is on a mission to find Christmas words. Can you help her?

MISTLETOE   NORTH POLE
CAROL   ELVES
GIFT   STOCKINGS
TREE   ORNAMENTS
SANTA CLAUS   HOLIDAY

3 Guide the caticorn to the top of the Christmas tree.

4 Help the caticorn count the Christmas decorations.

3   2   3   6   1   4

5. Help the caticorn get to the Christmas present.

6. What comes next?

7. Unscramble the words to complete the crossword.

Across
1. rohn
3. caitronc
6. irfay
7. nrtho lope
8. loracs
9. delcan
11. weom
13. vsele

Down
2. lophrud
3. chminye
4. nowairbs
5. yadolih
8. sioudc
10. lenag
12. loyjl

8. Use the color key to color the picture.

1 - Pink
2 - Purple
3 - Red
4 - Brown
5 - Blue
6 - Yellow
7 - Green
8 - Black
9 - White

 **9** Spot 5 differences between the pictures.

 **10** Write the correct symbol in each circle. Is it greater than, less than or equal to?

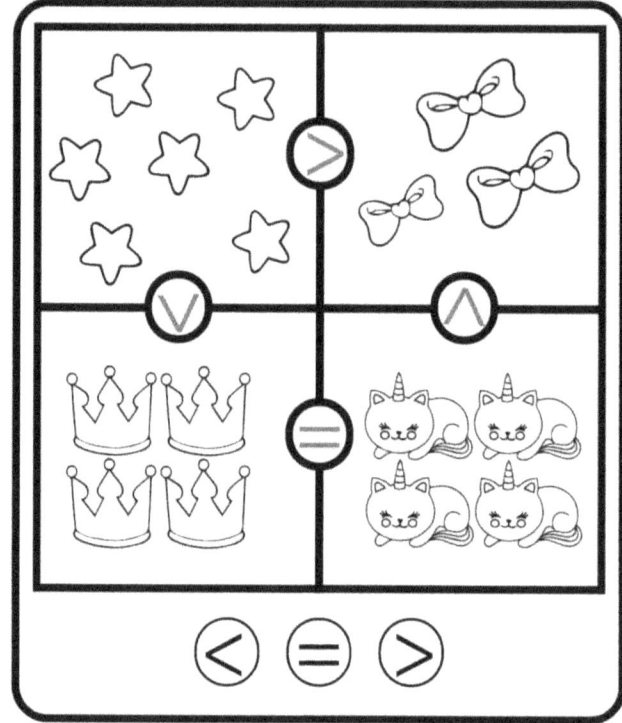

 **11** Find the words listed below.

 **12** Draw a line to help the caticorn match the Santa to its shadow.

MYSTICAL   CHRISTMAS   WINTER
SLEIGH   CATICORN   SNOWMAN
REINDEER   WHISKERS   BONBON
DECEMBER   GLITTER   TWINKLE

 **13** Connect the dots to complete the picture.

 **14** Can you solve the caticorn problem?

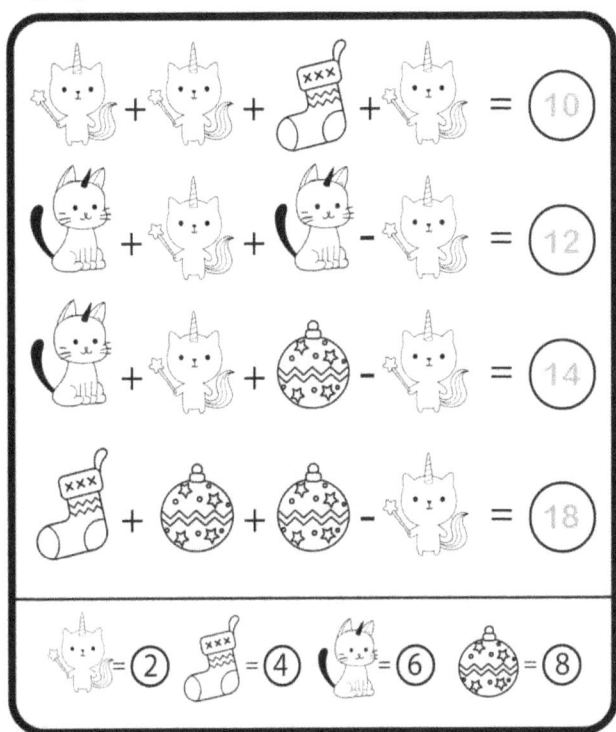

 **15** Spot 5 differences between the pictures.

 **16** The caticorn has dropped its Christmas hat. Can you help the caticorn find it?

 Use the color key to color the picture.

a - green
b - red
c - yellow
d - white
e - pink
f - orange
g - purple
h - brown

 Color the objects that repeat three times in a row.

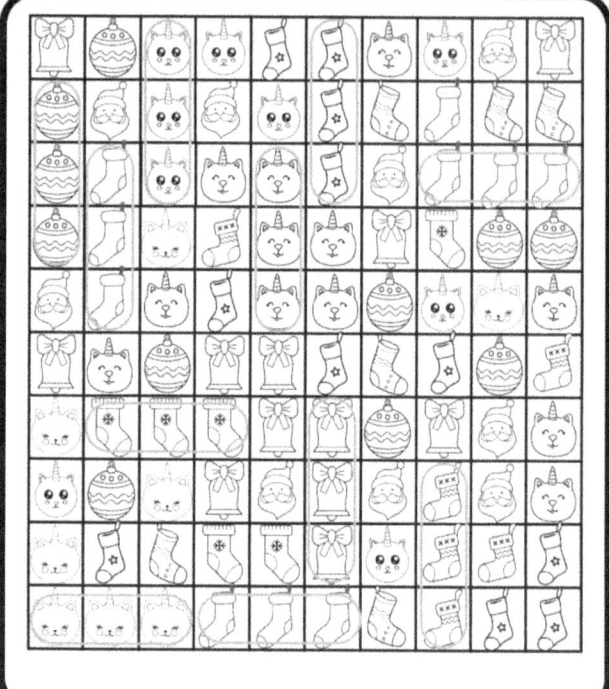

 Draw the missing parts to complete the caticorn's face.

 Count and color the correct number.

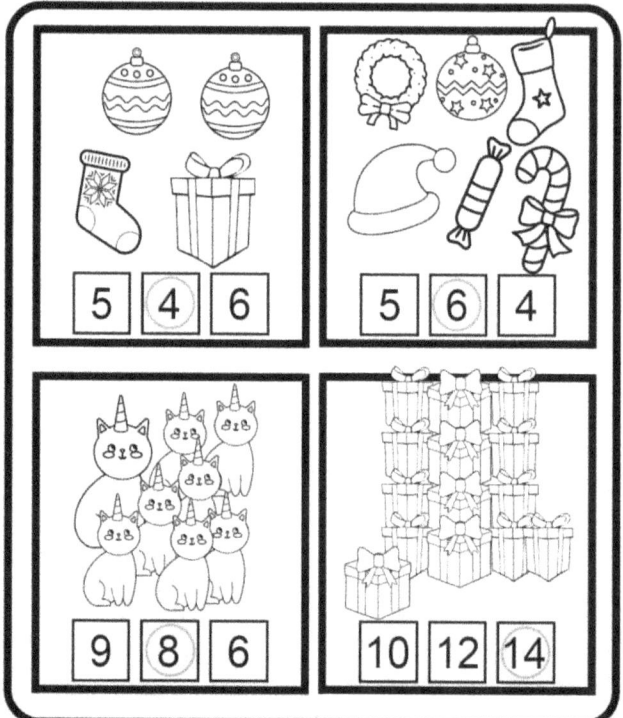

As a thank you for purchasing this book, enjoy these bonus pages from one of our other Christmas activity books!

1) Put the letters together to form a Christmas greeting.

☆☆☆☆☆
☆☆☆☆☆☆☆☆☆☆

 **2** Connect the dots to complete the picture.

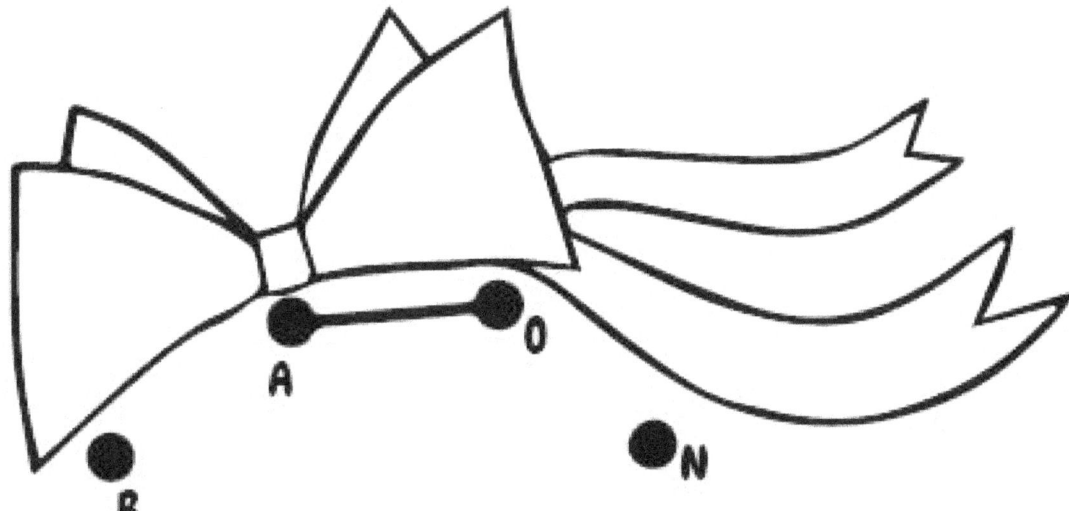

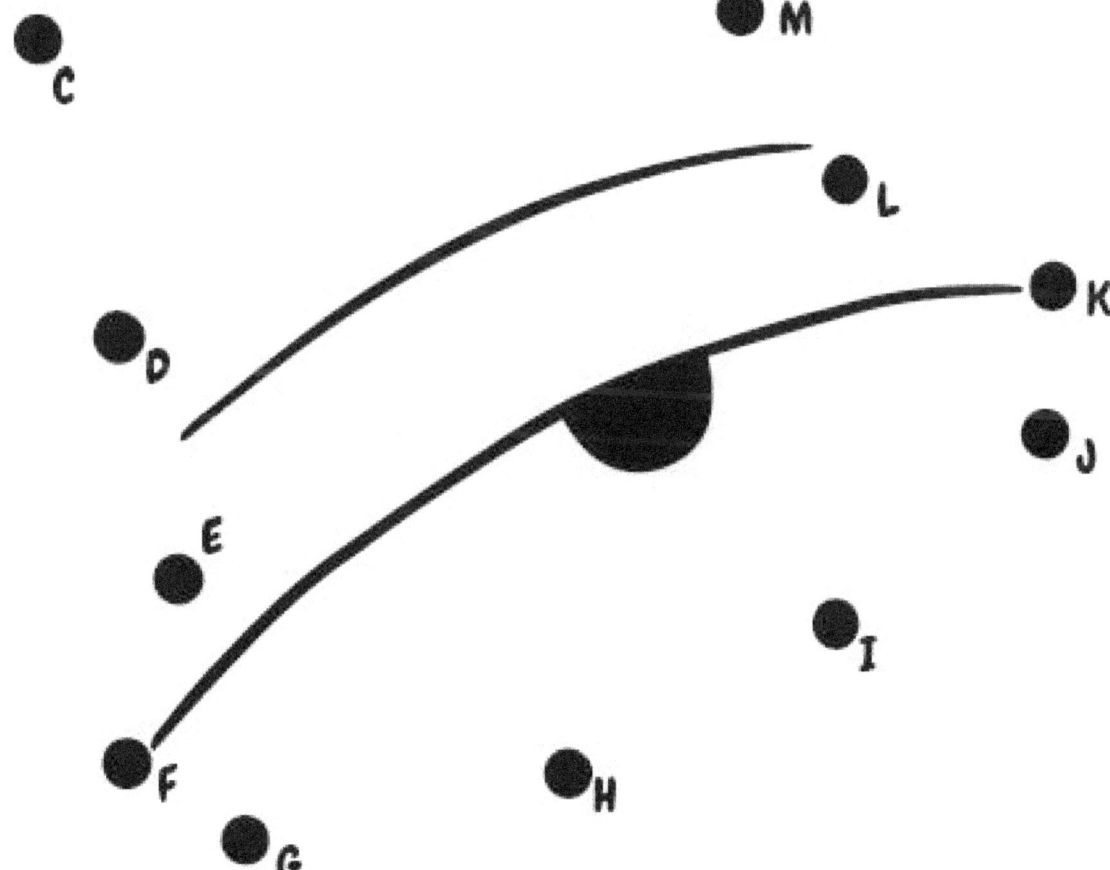

A Message From the Publisher

Hello! My name is Harper and I am the owner of Happy Harper Publishing, the publishing house that brought you this title.

My hope is that your little one loved this book and enjoyed each and every page. If they did, please think about leaving a review for us on Amazon or wherever you purchased this book. It may only take a moment, but it really does mean the world for small businesses like mine.

The mission of Happy Harper is to create premium content for children that will help them learn new things, grow their imaginations, improve their motor skills, and have lots of fun doing it. Without you, however, this would not be possible, so we sincerely thank you for your purchase and for supporting our company mission.

~ Harper

Check out our other books!

For more, visit our Amazon store at:
amazon.com/author/happyharper

www.ingramcontent.com/pod-product-compliance
Lightning Source LLC
LaVergne TN
LVHW060336080526
838202LV00053B/4483